W9-ARM-909

JANE GOODALL AND THE
WILD CHIMPANZEES

First Steck-Vaughn Edition 1992

Copyright © 1989 American Teacher Publications

Published by Steck-Vaughn Company

Library of Congress number: 89-3869

Library of Congress Cataloging in Publication Data.

Birnbaum, Bette.
  Jane Goodall and the wild chimpanzees / Bette Birnbaum; illustrated by Frederick Porter.

  (Real readers)
  Summary: A biography of the English zoologist, for beginning readers, describing her early experiences in Gombe, studying the wild chimpanzees.
  1. Goodall, Jane, 1934– —Juvenile literature. 2. Chimpanzees—Tanzania—Gombe Stream National Park—Juvenile literature. 3. Gombe Stream National Park (Tanzania)—Juvenile literature. 4. Zoologists—England—Biography—Juvenile literature. [1. Goodall, Jane, 1934– . 2. Zoologists. 3. Chimpanzees.] I. Title. II. Series.
  QL31.G58B57 1989   59T.092′4—dc19 [B] [92]   89-3869

ISBN 0-8172-3509-4   hardcover library binding

ISBN 0-8114-6709-0   softcover binding

    4 5 6 7 8 9 0   96 95 94 93 92

Jane Goodall
—and the—
Wild Chimpanzees

by Bette Birnbaum
illustrated by Frederick Porter

**RAINTREE
STECK-VAUGHN**
P U B L I S H E R S
The Steck-Vaughn Company

Austin, Texas

When Jane Goodall was little she lived in England. Jane liked to sit and look at cats and dogs and birds. But she dreamed of seeing wild animals. Jane dreamed of going to Africa. She wanted to see the wild animals there.

In 1957 Jane did get to go to Africa. There she met a man named Dr. Louis Leakey. Dr. Leakey was a scientist. He had come to Africa to study animal bones.

Jane helped Dr. Leakey and Dr. Leakey's wife, Mary. They looked for the bones of animals that had lived long, long ago.

Jane liked helping Dr. Leakey. When she had time she sat and looked at wild animals. She made notes about what she saw.

Dr. Leakey said to Jane, "I can see you like wild animals. I have a good job for you. This job means studying live, wild apes. Do you want this job? Do you want to go study wild chimpanzees?"

Jane said, "Yes! When can I go?"

8

Jane's job with the chimpanzees would take a long, long time. Dr. Leakey said that scientists wanted to find out about the life of chimpanzees in the wild. To do this Jane had to live in the wild. She had to see all the things that the chimpanzees did.

Jane liked to sit and look at animals. She liked to take notes. She would be good at this job.

In 1960 Jane went to Gombe in Tanzania, Africa. Lots of chimpanzees lived at Gombe. And for a long time that is where Jane lived, too.

Day in and day out Jane went looking for chimpanzees. She hiked on rocks. She went up and down hills. She got lots of bug bites and cuts. She looked and looked in the long grass.

But Jane did not see chimpanzees. When the chimpanzees saw Jane, they ran and hid.

Jane did not know what to do. She had to see the chimpanzees to study them!

Jane was not happy, but she did not stop looking for chimpanzees. On a good day, she hiked to the top of a hill. She sat down. She had a pad and a pen to make notes. She looked and looked for chimpanzees.

Jane looked and looked, but she did not see chimpanzees. She was thinking about going home to England. She looked down. What did she see?

Jane saw chimpanzees! Jane saw chimpanzees in the tops of trees. She saw chimpanzees eating figs!

The chimpanzees did not run. They let Jane look at them eating. Jane made notes about the chimpanzees as they ate and ate and ate!

In time, the chimpanzees got used to Jane. They let Jane sit and look at them doing lots and lots of things.

Jane liked being with the chimpanzees. She sat with the same chimpanzees day in and day out. She made notes about things like chimpanzee greetings. Jane noted that chimpanzees nod, pat, and yap in greeting. They hug and kiss, too!

Jane made notes about what wild chimpanzees like to eat. Chimpanzees eat things like bugs and figs. At times, they like to eat bits of meat. And they like bananas all of the time. A big male chimpanzee can eat 60 bananas at a time!

What does a chimpanzee do when the sun goes down? Jane made notes about that. A chimpanzee makes a "bed" of vines up in a tree.

Jane made notes about all the things that wild chimpanzees do.

She made notes about big chimpanzees. They used long grass to poke for bugs to eat. She made notes about little chimpanzees. They played games with vines. If a chimpanzee got ill and did not look well, Jane made notes about that, too.

As time went on, Jane picked names for the chimpanzees. She used the names of the chimpanzees in the notes she made.

David Greybeard was a big chimpanzee. David liked to take things that Jane had. He liked to take Jane's bananas and eat them. He liked to take pads and pens. David made off with Jane's pots and pans, too!

Mike was not big like David Greybeard, but he was the top male chimpanzee. The top chimpanzee is like a boss. Mike got to the top with lots of puffing and yelling. He would drum on boxes and cans. He would jump up and down. That made all the male chimpanzees run and hide. Mike was the boss!

Flo was the top female chimpanzee. She was the mother of 5 of the chimpanzees. Jane named Flo's little chimpanzees Faben, Figan, Fifi, Flint, and Flame.

Jane noted that Flo was a good mother. Flo let the little chimpanzees come in the bed she made. She gave them things to eat. And Flo played with the little chimpanzees. Fifi liked to tug at Flo's legs. Flint liked to ride on Flo's back.

Till Jane went to Gombe, scientists did not know about the life of chimpanzees in the wild. But now scientists have read Jane's books filled with findings. They have seen Jane on T.V. They know about David Greybeard, Mike, and Flo.

Jane helps scientists, and all of us, take a good look at wild chimpanzees and the homes they have in the wild.

Sharing the Joy of Reading

Beginning readers enjoy reading books on their own. Reading a book is a worthwhile activity in and of itself for a young reader. However, a child's reading can be even more rewarding if it is shared. This sharing can enhance your child's appreciation — both of the book and of his or her own abilities.

   Now that your child has read **Jane Goodall and the Wild Chimpanzees**, you can help extend your child's reading experience by encouraging him or her to:

- Retell the story or key concepts presented in this story in his or her own words. The retelling can be oral or written.

- Create a picture of a favorite character, event, or concept from this book.

- Express his or her own ideas and feelings about the subject of this book and other things he or she might want to know about this subject.

Here is an activity that you can do together to help extend your child's appreciation of this book: Encourage your child to observe an animal's behavior, like Jane Goodall did. Choose an animal, such as a family pet, an animal in the neighborhood, or an animal at a zoo. Sit quietly with your child and watch the animal. If you wish, you may both take notes as you watch. Afterwards, talk about what the animal looks like and what it did. Together, write several sentences describing one thing the animal did. Your child might like to draw a picture to accompany them.